CREATING
WITH
FLOWERS

INTERNATIONAL MASTERS PUBLISHERS INC.

Jug of Blooms page 13

contents

fresh flowers

silk flowers

dried flowers

introduction

As you turn the pages of this beautifully photographed how-to book, you will see how easy it is to create stunning flower displays and arrangements for your home and for any special occasion. Each project features full-color photos and easy-to-follow step-by-step instructions. A handy list of the flowers and materials needed are listed so you can gather everything you need before you begin. Plus, dozens of handy tips make the projects easy and enjoyable. Beautifully photographed project variation designs will be sure to show you what you are looking for and even spark your imagination for creating arrangements in your own style. Whether they're fresh cut, dried or silk flowers, you will find projects to suit all your needs. *Creating with Flowers* will impress and delight everyone from the least experienced to the most accomplished floral enthusiast.

Country Colors page 17

fresh flowers

Who can resist a big bouquet of fresh daisies, heralding the arrival

of summer? Or, a fragrant arrangement of deep red roses — the ultimate Valentine

seduction. Fresh flowers add so much to our lives. They brighten a

mood on a rainy afternoon. They complement a decorating style. They can

even say, "I'm sorry." Here, you will learn how to compose arrangements

both simple and intricate, using flowers from asters to zinnias. We'll show you

how to balance shape, color, even fragrance, to achieve just the

look and feel you want. So whether you need a get-well bouquet for a

friend, a hostess gift for an upcoming party, a centerpiece for a romantic

dinner, or just a way to show off those daisies from your garden,

start turning the pages to find creative new ideas.

Country Jug of Blooms

Dig that dusty old jug out from under your sink and put it to good use, brightening a dull spot in your home. Almost any combination of fresh flowers will work, but we've chosen tulips, forget-me-nots, hyacinths, and blossoms from cherry and almond trees. Choose a jug that is quite heavy as it will be less likely to tip over. Stoneware, glass, and porcelain are natural choices, and each would make a lovely country arrangement.

YOU WILL NEED

FLOWERS:

3 cherry blossom stems

8 almond blossom stems

2 stems viburnum

8 deep pink and pink-yellow ranunculi

5 pink tulips

8 forget-me-nots

8 blue-grape hyacinths

1 pink Dutch hyacinth

4 blue Dutch hyacinths

MATERIALS: Country-style jug, about 7 inches tall • Flower clippers
• Chicken wire, optional

KEYS TO SUCCESS

• If your favorite jug is cracked or is a nonwater-proof container, you can still use it. Fill a glass jar with water, and place it inside your jug. Then arrange flowers right in the glass jar.

• Woody stems, like those of the cherry, viburnum, and dogwood, have a tendency to cloud water faster than green stems. Therefore, if you are using a clear jug you should change the arrangement's water every day.

TIPS & TECHNIQUES

• It's the type of flower rather than the style and shape of the arrangement that makes a bouquet country-style. Avoid using formal or exotic flowers such as roses, lilies, or orchids.

1. Cut cherry, almond, and viburnum stems so that they are two-and-a-half times the height of jug. To improve water intake, make a vertical, ½ inch long slit at the end of each woody stem with a sharp knife.

2. If the flower heads are large and heavy, put a piece of chicken wire into neck of jug to support stems. Then, begin the arrangement by positioning the cherry, almond, and viburnum stems at the back of jug.

3. Trim hyacinths so that they will stand 3 to 5 inches taller than the jug's rim. Be sure the lower white part of each hyacinth stem is trimmed off to create a clear passageway for water. The place Dutch hyacinths at front of display

4. Divide the blue-grape hyacinths into two bunches. Position one bunch at the side of the jug and one bunch at the front of the jug. Tuck the clusters of forget-me-nots between the two bunches of hyacinths.

5. Place a pink Dutch hyacinth to the left of the display and position a short cherry blossom stem at the front-center of jug. Fill in gaps with tulips and ranunculi, spacing them evenly across the display.

SUNSET HUES

Country-style displays need not be comprised of pastel color, as evidenced by these vibrant bloomers. A colorful pitcher adds wonderful contrast to these sunset-inspired flowers:

- orange ranunculi
- orange lily-flowered tulips
- mauve tulips
- Queen Anne's lace
- purple lilacs
- chartreuse wood spurge
- lavender
- purple hellebores

COTTAGE GARDEN

Graceful yet simple cottage-garden blooms complement any decorating style. Experiment with an all-white arrangement with blooms from your own garden. This cottage-garden display was created using common garden shrubs, including:

- green hellebores
- green viburnums
- white lilacs
- cherry blossoms
- mock orange blossoms

Formal Pastels

Introduce the abundance and beauty of springtime into your home with this cheerful arrangement of fresh cut flowers. The pink hues of snapdragons, soft peach-colored tulips, and bright Stars-of-Bethlehem impart a warm, contemporary touch to a Sunday brunch, weekday luncheon, or an afternoon teatime table setting. In order to achieve the maximum effect, choose a tall, narrow vase of clear glass or crystal that slopes gently inward at the base.

YOU WILL NEED

FLOWERS:

10 deep pink and pale pink snapdragons

7 peach tulips

13 pink gladioli

9 Stars-of-Bethlehem

4 tuberoses

MATERIALS:
• Tall crystal vase • Scissors

1. Begin stripping the bottom leaves of the flower stems. Since foliage will decay if sitting underwater, be sure to strip all leaves that would otherwise fall below the vase's water line.

2. Add water to the vase. Hold the display's tallest flowers, the snapdragons, next to the vase. Cut snapdragons so that they are one-and-a-half times taller than the vase.

3. Begin positioning snapdragons so that the tallest points are on the right and left sides of the vase. Next, cut the gladioli so that they stand a few inches shorter than the snapdragons.

4. Position the gladioli at the front of the vase. Begin adding Stars-of-Bethlehem and tuberoses to sides of display. The curved blooms of both flowers provide a nice contrast for the upright, linear flowers.

5. The flowers should lead the eye from the tallest point of one side of the vase, down, then back up to the tallest point of the other side. Softly accent the arrangement with large-cupped tulips.

CLEVER IDEAS

The tall flower stems used in this arrangement are the perfect height for accenting napkins. Right before guests arrive, roll up a silk napkin so that it is cylindrical and place a gladiolus stem on top. Secure the pastel bloom to the napkin with a gold cord.

SPECIAL THOUGHTS

Honor a special woman on Mother's Day or her birthday with an arrangement from the heart. Let her know that you chose flowers that matched her style! This formal arrangement of baby pinks and yellows is accented with pristine white lilies. To replicate this bouquet you will need:

- pastel yellow stocks
- pink stocks
- pink larkspurs
- white calla lilies
- white Easter lilies

COUNTRY COLORS

A classy collection of "true blue" blooms makes a splash of color on any window's ledge. Continue the color theme right down to the container. Here we grounded our arrangement with a clear blue vase. Our floral shades of blue include:

- deep blue irises
- light blue delphiniums
- deep wine delphiniums
- lavender blue stocks

Rose Wedding Centerpiece

Roses are the universal symbol of love, so what better flowers to choose for a wedding celebration centerpiece? This lush arrangement includes all the best the rose family has to offer, from the delicate peach blooms of "Osiana" to the vibrant hue of the bright pink "Hotspot." The bride and groom will remember this lovely gift for years to come. And almost as memorable as the spectacular beauty this bountiful arrangement will provide, is the lush fragrance it gives off.

YOU WILL NEED

FLOWERS:

5 caspia stems

12 "Dolores" roses
(medium pink)

10 "Osiana" roses
(pale peach)

12 "Marlyse" roses
(pale pink)

8 "Hotspot" roses
(bright pink)

2 pink spray roses

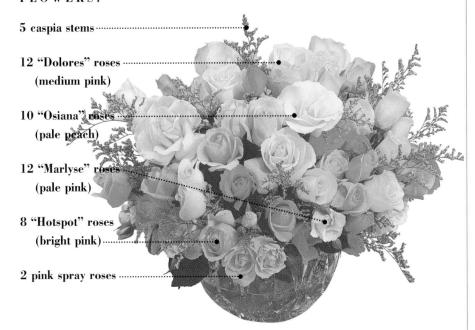

MATERIALS: Glass bowl • Floral foam for fresh flowers • Florist's spike • Tacky adhesive • Glass flower marbles

1. Secure a block of presoaked floral foam in your bowl with a florist's spike and tacky adhesive. Add marbles to the bowl to provide weight and to hide the floral foam.

2. Place about seven roses in an arc across the center of the floral foam. The flower in the center will be the highest point of the arrangement. Start by alternating the peach roses with the lighter pinks.

3. Place the rest of the lighter tints into the arrangement, starting at the center and working outward. Insert stems into the floral foam gently, making sure they don't bend in the process.

4. Once you've placed all of the lighter pink roses, begin inserting the brightest roses into the foam. Space them evenly throughout, following the round shape of the display.

5. Finish the display by tucking in sprigs of caspia. Use extra green foliage from the roses if you need to fill in any gaps. Check the floral foam and add water to the bowl as necessary.

CLEVER IDEAS

Save fallen rose petals that may have come loose while you were working. Put them in a basket and have the flower girl sprinkle a path of petals as she leads the bride down the aisle. What better way to usher in a rosy life for the newlyweds?

SEASONAL LOOK

For the autumn bride, create a rose center-piece that echoes the vibrant, yet romantic, colors of the season. A beautiful crystal vase adds a touch of formality suited for a grand wedding celebration. We chose these roses for their dense, bright colors:

- "Mme. Delbard" (deep red)
- "Raphaela" (lighter red)
- "Marela" (creamy orange)
- "Pareo" (lighter orange)

EVENING DELIGHT

For an evening wedding, an elegant white display will be visible even when the lights are low. The tightly closed buds of the roses gives the arrangement style and grace. The deep rich green of the box holly complements the delicate white tulips. Two varieties of tulips add interesting appeal:

- "Carte Blanc" (white)
- "White Bridal"(blush)
- sprigs of box holly

Table for Two Candlestick

Soft lighting. Romantic music. A sumptuous dinner. Now all you need is a centerpiece to match the mood. Here it is, a candle transformed by fragrant roses and cascading leaves of ivy. Don't worry if your dinner is scheduled for this evening because we have good news: once you have assembled all the supplies for the project, you will be able to create the centerpiece in about 15 minutes. And that leaves more time for romance.

YOU WILL NEED

FLOWERS:

18 peach-tipped
yellow roses

1 bunch
sweet Melissa

12 stems of
variegated ivy

MATERIALS: Candlestick • Candlestick cup for holding foam • Floral foam for fresh flowers • Knife • Scissors

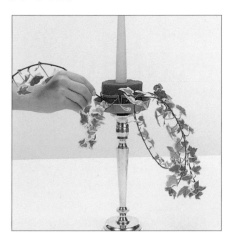

1. Insert floral cup into candlestick, securing it with tacky adhesive if necessary. Use a knife to cut down floral foam to fit into the cup. Gently press the foam into the holder.

2. Push the candle into foam until it's secure. If necessary, cut a hole into the foam to accommodate the candle. Add water to the cup's water basin which will keep the foam moist.

3. Trim the ivy stems so that they are 5 to 8 inches long. If the candlestick is quite tall, cut longer trails of ivy to curl around the candlestick. Place ivy stems around the base of the floral foam.

CLEVER IDEAS

For a toast to a love that's evergreen, set the table with the floral candlestick. Then, wind a single tendril of ivy around the neck of a champagne or wine bottle and along the stems of your favorite glasses.

4. Cut rose stems to 2 inch lengths. Insert roses just above the ivy stems, working in tiers until you reach the top of the foam. For best results, roses shouldn't cover up more than half the height of the candle.

5. Fill in gaps between roses with sweet Melissa stems. You may have to trim the stems to fit the height of the candlestick. Insert the shortest stems near top of display. Mist display with water to keep it looking fresh.

SPECIAL CELEBRATION

Celebrate your wedding anniversary with a special centerpiece designed with flowers similar to those used in your wedding bouquet. Most any flower or green will work well in this type of arrangement and, if watered well, will last for days. Ideal for casting an intimate glow on a silver anniversary, this candlestick arrangement is packed full of:

- ranunculi
- garden roses
- heather

BOLD COLOR

Ignite passion and romance to any dinner party with this candlestick arrangement of royal purples and striking magentas. A matching candle shows off the flowers dramatic faces. The jewel-like hues shown here are supplied by:

- red poppy anemones
- purple poppy anemones
- creamy orange ranunculi
- purple veronicas

silk flowers

Who says you can't fool mother nature? The beautiful silk flower

arrangements we offer here just may do the trick. It used to be we felt a little guilty

about using silk flowers in arrangements. But who among us hasn't

dreamed on a dull, cold wintery afternoon of a garden packed full of red, yellow,

and orange tulips, their blooms dancing in an early spring breeze? Or,

who hasn't longed to place a colorful arrangement of lilacs on a kitchen counter in

February? Silk flowers allow us to enjoy the colors, shapes, and

textures of fresh cut blooms all year long. With the projects that follow you won't

have a single regret of displaying silk flowers.

A Blooming Basket

In days gone by, women would rise early on a spring day and visit their cutting garden. There they would gather great armfuls of fresh picked flowers, arrange them in simple baskets, and carry them indoors, where they would brighten up a kitchen or sitting room. Our bountiful basket of silk flowers—brimming with bright tulips, dramatic Black-eyed Susans, and deep pink lilacs—allows you to bring that "fresh-from-the-garden" feeling indoors and enjoy it all year round.

YOU WILL NEED

FLOWERS:

3 yellow tulips

4 forsythia stems

6 deep pink lilacs

6 sprays black-eyed Susans

6 purple lilacs

1 bunch ferns

MATERIALS: Round basket, 9 inches wide and 6 inches high • Wire cutters • Sharp knife for cutting foam • Floral foam for dried flowers

1. Cut the floral foam into small blocks that fit snugly into the basket. Place tulips in an arc across the basket's center. These flowers will have the most height and will be the focal point of the display.

2. Place the lilacs in between the tulips to fill in the arc. Make sure the lilacs are not higher than the tulips. The bushy lilacs add fullness to the arrangement and their color makes a pleasing contrast with the tulips.

3. Starting at the center and working outward, place the Black-eyed Susans and forsythias into the floral foam. The forsythia should fill in the gaps between the tulips and lilacs.

4. Arrange the deep pink lilacs around the lowest edge of the arrangement to accent the display. Adding this third color will create a harmonious blend between the contrasting yellow tulips and purple lilacs.

5. For a finishing touch, insert a few ferns throughout the arrangement, filling in any empty spaces that remain among the flowers. Place arrangement in its permanent location and fill in any more gaps.

CLEVER IDEAS

Brighten any small area, such as bookshelves, a desk or bathrooms, by arranging the silk flowers in miniature baskets. These small-scale blooming baskets will add a pretty touch to any dark corner.

VARIATIONS

TEA PARTY BLOOMS

Treat weekend house guests to a Sunday brunch blooming with a basket of springtime favorites. A long wicker basket is the perfect container for silk blooms in colors that match your teapot and cups. The tea party blooms shown here are:

- pothos
- yellow roses, freesias and carnations
- white lilacs
- purple asters
- white miniature irises
- creamy yellow miniature irises
- magenta-edged, white morning glories

RUSTIC COTTAGE CHARM

Choose a rustic wooden basket with an unfinished twig handle to create an arrangement that replicates the wonderful feeling of springtime in the woods. Loosely pack the basket with flowers to give it a natural look. This display shows off:

- larkspurs
- burgundy snowball lilacs
- Japanese maple
- aralia branches
- hydrangeas

Gift Package Bouquet

Everyone loves receiving presents, but sometimes it can be a challenge thinking of new ways to make the presentation more special. The answer? A bright floral bouquet: a special reminder of the day on which it was given. Even a plain paper wrapping transforms into something special with this beautiful floral arrangement. It's the perfect touch for weddings, showers, birthdays, holidays—any occasion.

YOU WILL NEED

FLOWERS:

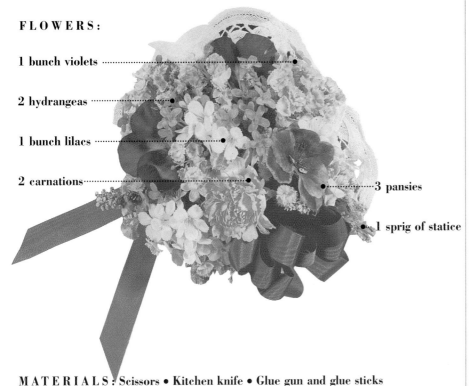

1 bunch violets

2 hydrangeas

1 bunch lilacs

2 carnations

3 pansies

1 sprig of statice

MATERIALS : Scissors • Kitchen knife • Glue gun and glue sticks
Lace doily • Florist's tape sticks • 1 yard ribbon wire

KEYS TO SUCCESS

● Insert the doily base into a bud vase or a drinking glass. This will not only keep both hands free, it will also keep the bouquet stable as you glue in the flowers.

● Affix your gift package bouquet to your gift-wrapped package with tacky adhesive. The adhesive will firmly hold the bouquet in place without ripping the wrapping paper when the bouquet is removed from the package.

TIPS & TECHNIQUES

● For an attractive finishing touch, wind some extra ribbon around the bouquet handle. This will hide the florist's tape and give the package bouquet a classic look.

1. Fold lace doily in half, then in half again. Cut off about ¼ inch at point to make a small hole in center of doily. Bunch together a few sprigs of German statice with florist's tape to form bouquet handle.

2. Push the handle through the hole of the doily. Apply glue to the underside of the statice stems. Glue the doily to the statice stems, firmly pinching the doily at intervals to create a gathered "collar."

3. Dab hot glue on 2- to 3-inch long lilac, hydrangea, and violet stems and begin inserting them into the statice base. These compact, densely packed flower stems will form the foundation of your bouquet.

4. Accent the bouquet by gluing in pansies and carnations. To make the bow, first cut 1 yard of ribbon in half lengthwise. Form a loop of desired size, looping the ribbon away from you.

5. Loop ribbon toward you to make a second, same-sized loop. Repeat until desired number of bow loops are completed. Wire center of bow tightly and crunch loops together so bow looks full. Insert into bouquet.

CLEVER IDEAS

A silk bouquet turns an ordinary gift bag into an extra-special gift wrapping. Simply make the package bouquet on a smaller scale and affix it to a gift bag with tacky adhesive. This is also a clever way to hide a small imperfection in a recycled gift bag.

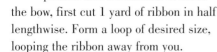

WEDDING SHOWER

A bridal shower or wedding is the perfect time to decorate a gift package with flowers that have special meaning—roses for love, carnations for affection, and lavender for devotion. Here we chose the following blooms for a lovely silk keepsake:

- roses
- carnations
- freesias
- lavender

A SPECIAL VALENTINE

Make your favorite Valentine feel even more special and attach a homemade rose nosegay to your Valentine's Day gift. It is super easy to make and will last longer than a dozen roses. Here, a doily base with elegant silk ribbon holds blossoms of:

- miniature roses
- baby's breath
- dried fern

Festive Poinsettias

If you have been searching for new ways to make your home more festive, look no further. You can make this one-of-a-kind holiday arrangement in under an hour. It is perfect atop a mantelpiece, a bookshelf, even as a Christmas or hostess gift. Either silk or fresh poinsettias will work, but if you choose live poinsettia plants, be sure to keep them away from pets and children because the plants can make them ill.

YOU WILL NEED

FLOWERS:

20 plastic pine sprigs

5 small pinecones, real or plastic

1 poinsettia plant with 7 blossoms

7 stems of white dwarf lilacs

MATERIALS: Wire cutters • Scissors • 1 block floral foam for dried flowers • 21 floral picks • 22-gauge wire • 2 yards of ribbon

KEYS TO SUCCESS

● Because this is a mantel-piece arrangement, the back will be relatively bare. If the weight of the flowers in the front makes your arrangement lean forward, place a rock or a small bag of rice toward the back of the foam to keep the display from toppling over.

● Snip the stems of plastic flowers at an angle so that they'll be easier to insert into the floral foam. Or, slide the stems over a bar of damp soap to lubricate them.

TIPS & TECHNIQUES

● Before cutting the foam base, be sure to measure the width of your mantel. Cut the base $1/4$ inch shorter than the maximum width.

● Also, if placing the arrange-ment over a fireplace that is used often, keep it to the side, not in the center over the heat of an open hearth.

1. Silk poinsettias are usually sold grouped together on one plant, so it will be necessary to snip each stem off with wire cutters. Cut 4 stems for sides to about 4 inches and 3 for top to about 7 inches.

2. Insert the poinsettia stems into the top of the floral foam and the shorter stems into the front and sides. Space the flower heads evenly, except for the back of the arrangement, which won't be seen.

3. Trim the ends of the dwarf lilac stems and begin inserting them into the floral foam. Place lilacs in the display at varying intervals to create a nice balance in color and texture with the poinsettias.

CLEVER IDEAS

For an informal get-together, hang colorful ball ornaments from the display to catch the light of an open fire below. If you are hosting a dinner party, consider placing a strand of white lights into the arrangement for a festive sparkle.

4. Attach floral picks to pine sprigs with wire. Then wire pinecone bases to pine sprigs, hiding the wire from view. Insert sprigs with cones into the foam, filling out the arrangement.

5. Make a bow with the 2 yards of ribbon and attach a floral pick to the center with wire. Stick the floral pick in the front of the arrangement, so the bow is a little off to the right side.

A HOLIDAY DAZZLER

For a dazzling mantelpiece arrangement that sets a festive mood, spray silk materials lightly with metallic gold spray paint. Use enough spray paint to create a gilded effect, allowing some of the original color to show through. Use a variety of textured material for the most stunning display. This gilded arrangement uses:

- sprays of magnolia leaves
- silk pomegranate branches
- winterberry branches

SHAPELY ALTERNATIVE

For a softer more casual look, opt for round blossoms of nontraditional holiday flowers in sweet pinks and whites. Adorn the festive arrangement with gold ribbon and traditional holiday greens. Recreate our soft arrangement using:

- pink queen roses
- pink-tipped white peonies
- spiranthes
- a variety of greens

Silk Triangular Display

Bold and beautiful, this unusual silk arrangement offers an alternative to customary round-shape displays. The peonies' generous proportions coupled with the distinct, angular lines of the lilies lend this arrangement an artistic feel. To achieve a well-balanced arrangement, choose a short, round container with a simple design, one that will complement, not compete with the boldly colored, highly textured flowers.

YOU WILL NEED

FLOWERS:

2 mauve liatris

3 to 6 yellow lilies

2 fuchsia peonies

4 sprigs of ivy

2 yellow freesias

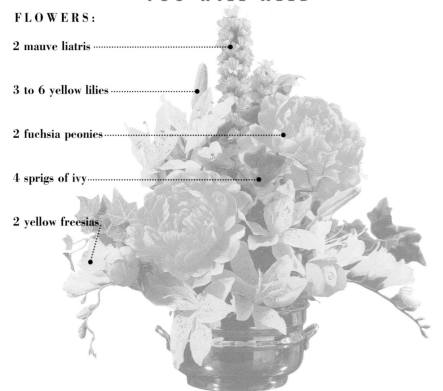

MATERIALS: Round container • Plastic foam base • Wire cutters • Kitchen knife • Felt-tip marker

KEYS TO SUCCESS

● Make sure the foam base fits snugly in its container. If it is too loose, the arrangement could tilt or easily pop out. Use tacky adhesive and a florist's spike for extra hold.

● Because this is a flatbacked display, concentrate flowers in the front and sides. Do not leave the back completely bare, however, or your arrangement will appear two dimensional.

TIPS & TECHNIQUES

● Silk flowers have wires and are very malleable. Once all of the flowers have been inserted, take advantage of this feature by bending flower heads to fill in gaps in the arrangement.

1. Place container upside down on foam base and trace around rim with felt-tip marker. Trim foam with knife, making it a little smaller than outline, but wide enough so that it fits snugly in the container.

2. Place the stems of liatris in the center of the foam base, making one taller than the other. Next, bend each freesia stem at a 90° angle and insert them into either side of the arrangement.

3. Soften the angular line you have created by placing one peony to the front and one peony to the upper left side of the display. If peony stems have buds, snip these off and arrange them as separate flowers.

4. Fill in the triangle by adding lilies—bending the stems to make them look real. Place the lilies at the front and sides—since this is a flat-backed display, it's not necessary to fill in the back.

5. Tuck sprigs of ivy in between the flowers in the front and sides of container. The greens should not be higher than the flowers, but should be visible enough to complement the larger flower heads.

CLEVER IDEAS

An extra silk bloom makes a simple but lovely bookmark for a growing reading list. Embellish the stems with a colorful ribbon or extra silk leaves.

AUTUMNAL GLOW

Bring the fiery hues of autumn indoors with this vibrant, ever-lasting arrangement of oranges and reds. Shades of orange and red complement one another, replicating the wonderful colors of fall foliage. Consider adding some dried colored leaves to the display for a natural accent. This striking arrangement proudly displays:

- red dahlias
- orange lilies
- yellow freesias

HOLIDAY MAKEOVER

Color your Christmas with an arrangement in various shades of red that captures the festiveness of the season. The vibrant arrangement shown here proves that there is more to Christmas flowers than poinsettias. Three beautiful blooms make up this arrangement:

- burnt red hydrangeas
- red amaryllis
- red freesias

Summery Table Garland

Forget about the usual basket-of-fruit centerpiece. Jazz up the entire table at your next warm-weather party with this cool-hued garland. With its dazzling combination of Black-eyed Susans, yarrow and lilacs, the garland makes the perfect table accent because it adds a splash of color and its low height allows for unobstructed conversation between guests. Store the garland in tissue paper to have on hand whenever you need to add color to your table.

YOU WILL NEED

FLOWERS:

4 yellow yarrows

11 Black-eyed Susans

6 double-headed purple lilacs

6 multi-blossomed strawflowers

1 bunch of lilac leaves

15 purple asters

4 snowball lilacs

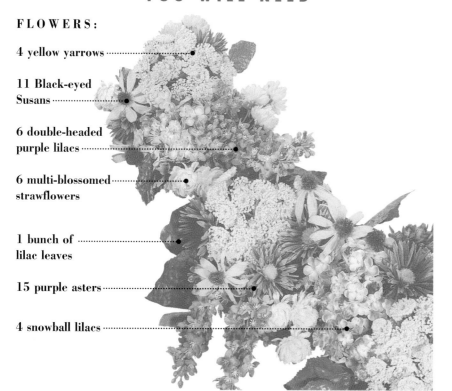

MATERIALS: 2 raffia braids or bag of raffia to braid • Glue gun and glue sticks • Wire cutters • Florist's wire

KEYS TO SUCCESS

● To make braids, tie long strands of raffia to a sturdy support so that braid will be well anchored. Divide strands by hand into three equal pieces, then alternately braid left and right sections with the center one. Continue until you have completed a 1 to 2 foot long braid. Cut and knot the end with another piece of raffia, leaving a 2 to 3 inch tail.

TIPS & TECHNIQUES

● To give dimension to the garland, cut flowers to varying heights; cut some completely down while leaving others with 1 to 2 inch stems. Once greens are glued, individual leaves may need to be twisted by hand to face forward or positioned so that they better fill in any gaps.

1. Line up two 1 to 2 feet raffia braids side by side with tails facing away from each other. Position the braids so that, when lined up, they have equally long ends. Wire braids into position to create garland base.

2. Begin positioning leaves to face out in different directions along the length of the garland, leaving enough room for flowers to be inserted. Apply glue to bottoms of leaves and affix them to garland.

3. Establish the design by carefully placing the four yarrows along the garland so that they are spaced out evenly. Once you're pleased with their placement, glue them into place.

4. Balance out the bright yellow hues of the yarrows by adding purple flowers. Start by gluing the clusters of lilacs to the garland and then offset their fullness with the addition of daisy-like asters.

5. Fill in gaps with small, singular gold blooms (strawflowers and Black-eyed-Susans), dabbing them with glue before inserting them into garland. Glue a few of these blooms right to the leaves for visual interest.

CLEVER IDEAS

For a coordinating table accent, design a small-scale garland to wind around the outside of a punch bowl. Use smaller foliage to cover raffia base and divide lilac and yarrow clusters into thirds to keep garland in proportion to the size of punch bowl. Affix to punch bowl with double-sided adhesive tape and tie garland ends together with wire.

MEXICAN FIESTA

Spice up your Mexican dinner with a garland that boasts a fiesta of vibrant colors. Extend the Mexican theme by decorating a party piñata with extra flowers and chili peppers. This festive garland is made of:

- blue dahlias
- yellow chrysanthemums
- deep pink rhododendron clusters
- orange dahlias
- orange chrysanthemums

SPECIAL CELEBRATION

Say "Aloha" to Hawaiian luau partygoers with this tropical garland. As evidenced by the lilies and irises in this garland, you don't need to search out rare island flowers for this project—a simple mix of everyday silk flowers can often create an exotic, tropical feel by themselves.

- stargazer lilies
- large yellow irises
- ferns

Garden-Inspired Mirror

Don't wait for the warm weather to enjoy nature's floral colors in your home. With a little creativity, and some simple silk flowers, you can recreate a colorful summer garden, complete with a picket fence and wicker mirror, in your home. And no matter where you choose to hang this mirror—in a guest room, a bathroom, or a hallway—each time you pass this bright spot you'll be reminded of the beauty of the garden outdoors.

YOU WILL NEED

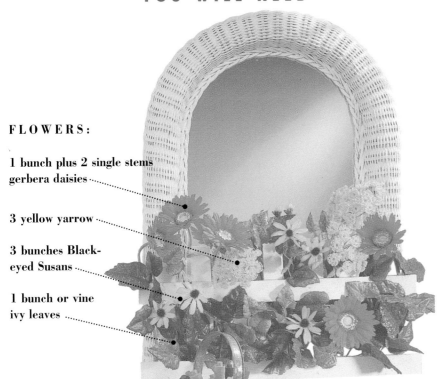

FLOWERS:

1 bunch plus 2 single stems gerbera daisies

3 yellow yarrow

3 bunches Black-eyed Susans

1 bunch or vine ivy leaves

MATERIALS: Wicker mirror • Picket fence • Two ³/₄ inch nails • Hammer • Handsaw • Sandpaper • White spray paint • Glue gun and gluesticks

KEYS TO SUCCESS

● Glue flowers onto the picket fence, not the mirror, in case you decide to update the design for a different season or another room in your house. Simply lift off the picket fencing, carefully put in storage, and replace with a new alternate design.

● Measure the mirror you choose carefully before purchasing it to make sure it is tall enough for the fencing. Keep in mind you might have to trim the fence both horizontally and vertically to fit.

TIPS & TECHNIQUES

● To save yourself time, when purchasing the picket fence piece for the project, ask your home center to trim it to the mirror's dimensions. Most home centers and hardware stores will perform this type of service free of charge.

1. Spray the picket fence and the wicker border of the mirror with white spray paint and allow paint to dry before continuing. For extra protection, place masking tape around mirror edges before spraying.

2. Measure the fence to fit the width of the mirror and, if necessary, cut off excess wood with a handsaw. Attach fence to the bottom of the mirror frame by gently hammering a nail to either side. Sand down rough edges.

3. Place the gerbera daisies in first, tucking their stems through the slats in the fence with a small dab of glue to hold in place. Place two flowers on the right side of the fence and the cluster on the upper left.

4. Insert yarrow stems into fence, placing two of the flowers near the higher gerbera daisy on the right and one below the triplet of daisies on the left. Insert yarrow stems into fence, then trim the stem if necessary.

5. Place Black-eyed Susans on the lower left side of the frame and two on top near the middle. Then finish by artfully tucking the ivy leaves through the fence, covering spaces between slats.

CLEVER IDEAS

Carry the garden theme to another wall of your room by adorning a hand fork or trowel with extra silk blooms. Antique garden tools, highlighted with a delicate silk flower, make fun and whimsical room decor and wall hangings. Be sure tools are placed out of reach of children.

A SPRING GARDEN

You don't need a green thumb for this garden-inspired mirror. A painted trellis blooming with pastel spring-like flowers is perfect for brightening up a sunroom or guest bedroom. This mirror uses silk blooms of:

- yellow tulips
- yellow snap dragons
- periwinkle lilac sprays
- Queen Anne's lace
- yellow pansy sprays
- purple pansy sprays
- ferns

STYLISH ALTERNATIVE

Rambling silk roses and climbing ivy inter-twined around the border of a mirror create a natural-looking garden trellis with just a hint of romance. The wicker-framed mirror gives the mirror a casual appearance. For a more formal room, use a wood framed mirror. Perfect for a powder room, this mirror showcases:

- light pink climbing rose vines
- ivy vines

dried flowers

Deeply colored and beautiful textured dried flower arrangements provide a feeling that is reminiscent of nature's bounty. But unlike their fresh-flower counterparts, the beauty of dried flower arrangements lasts months and months, sometimes even years. And even better, you no longer need an enormous cutting garden or lots of spare room to dry fresh flowers: you'll find everything you need at most crafts shops. Year-round, most craft stores offer hundreds of dried flowers—in every shape, color and texture imaginable—offering you endless possibilities for creating just the right flower arrangement for your home. However, don't let the flowers at the craft store stop you from growing your own cut-flower garden. Drying flowers is easy, especially if you follow our special tips at the back of the book.

A Welcome Wreath

Floral wreaths conjure images of warm welcomes and hospitality, and this one, made from dried flowers, is no exception. Crisp white daisies and assorted golden grasses add country charm to the wreath, but its bright colors and bold ribbon lend a contemporary feel that fits any decor. But be warned: These wreaths are so easy to make, you may not be able to stop! Which may be a good thing, since this charmer makes a terrific gift.

YOU WILL NEED

FLOWERS:

10 assorted grasses

3 cockscombs

3 hydrangeas

16 pink larkspurs

15 yellow daisies

4 poppy pods

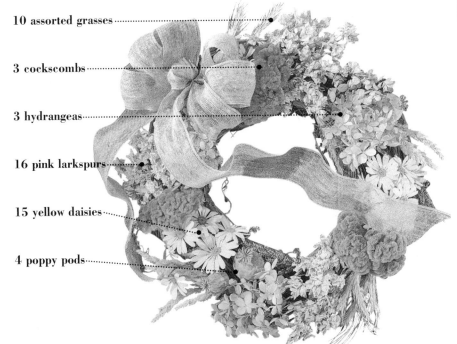

MATERIALS: 2 yards wired ribbon • 12-inch grapevine wreath base • Glue gun and glue sticks • Floral wire • Scissors

1. Cut each cockscomb stem down to about 2 inches. Dab stem ends with hot glue and insert into the grapevine wreath base. Place the three flower heads about equal distances apart from each other on the base.

2. Dab poppy pods with hot glue and insert into wreath in pairs between cockscomb flower heads. (Save a space between two of the cockscombs for the bow.) Nestle the assorted dried grasses into wreath between cockscomb.

3. Trim off stems of daisies. Group them in clusters and glue them next to the cockscomb flower heads. Glue hydrangea clusters near the poppy pods. Let wreath sit for 5 minutes to allow glue to set.

4. Trim each larkspur stem to about 5 inches before gluing them in clusters around wreath. Stand back and look at wreath, making any adjustments before the glue is completely dry.

5. With 2 yards of wired ribbon, make a multi-looped bow and attach it to the front of the wreath with a few inches of floral wire. Gently crimp the ribbon tails of the bow to form subtle curves.

CLEVER IDEAS

Create this dried flower wreath as an ornament that is perfect for hanging on gift bottles or a country-style Christmas tree. Simply glue scraps of dried flowers to a tiny grapevine wreath and hang with a narrow pastel ribbon.

TABLETOP WREATH

What happens when every room in your home already has a wreath? Make another and use it as a table accent! Any dried flower wreath takes on a new look when it's used to decorate a table. Match the flowers with the color scheme of a room and place the wreath on a table near a window so the flowers catch the natural light. This colorful wreath uses flowers in shades of yellow and purple:

- freesia
- larkspur
- alstromeria

SUMMERY WELCOME

A simple wreath, loaded with bright blooms, captures the sunny mood of lazy summer days. The large fabric bow, festively adorned with sunflowers, makes the perfect finishing touch, accenting the wreath's cheery color scheme. In addition to the basic wreath-making supplies (a base, glue gun and glue stick, wire, ribbon and scissors), you'll need:

- Black-eyed Susans
- wild peppergrass
- lemon leaves

Fragrant Mirror Swag

Fragrant green eucalyptus leaves combine with charming hydrangeas and delicate larkspurs in this attractive, simple-to-make swag, perfect for adorning any mirror in your home. And whether you only hang it for special occasions, or to brighten up a room any day of the year, this stylish and stunning swag will elicit compliments from family and friends. Make more than one and hang a swag over a fireplace mantel, a bright kitchen window, or even on the wall above your bed. Its eye-catching mixture of colors and textures will make a great addition to any room.

YOU WILL NEED

FLOWERS:

10 stems of
green eucalyptus

2 hydrangea
heads

18 pink
larkspurs

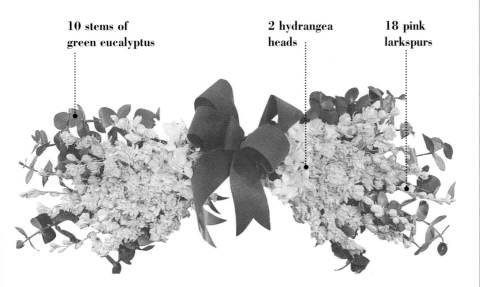

MATERIALS: Florist's wire • Glue gun and glue sticks • Scissors
3 yards of ribbon

1. To make an 18-inch long swag, begin by cutting ten eucalyptus stems to 9 inch lengths. Spread out five stems in a fan shape and then wire their stems together. Repeat this with the remaining five stems.

2. Bring the two fanshaped bunches together at their bases to form a "bow tie." Make sure both sides are symmetrical in shape and that the eucalyptus stems are lying fairly flat. Wire the two together where their stems meet.

3. Braid three pieces of 5 inch long florist's wire together to form a sturdy hanging loop for the swag. Attach loop to back of swag with wire. Bend loop so it can hook over and hang on a nail at back of mirror.

CLEVER IDEAS

If you know a bride-to-be, a simple mirror adorned with a miniature swag in her wedding colors makes a wonderful keepsake gift. Use left-over project material to make it. Use plenty of hot glue to secure the swag to the mirror.

4. Trim larkspurs so that they're 1 to 2 inches shorter than eucalyptus stems. Position nine larkspurs to either side of swag in a fanlike pattern and, once pleased with placement, glue them to eucalyptus.

5. At the base of each larkspur glue a hydrangea head. With 3 yards of ribbon, tie a multi-looped bow. Position bow to hide glue, wire, and stem ends. Bend wire around the middle of bow and swag.

NATURAL CHOICE

Brighten up that old wood mirror with a lively colored swag. The magnificent colors of autumn are reflected in wonderful dried flowers, collected fallen leaves, and golden autumn grasses. A deep rich bow ties the vibrant colors together with the dark rich frame. The natural choices shown here are:

- bare blueberry bush branches
- oak leaves
- strawflowers
- wheat stalks or dried grass spikes

SIMPLE AND SWEET

Strands from a simple raffia bow complement this plain and simple country swag. Placing the swag on the wall above the mirror makes the mirror appear taller. To match our dried swag shown here, use tawny, sage green, and dusty mauve hues such as:

- seeded eucalyptus branches
- rye spikes
- proteas

Elegant Urn Display

A mix of reds and pinks burst from a simple white urn in this dramatic arrangement. Its height makes this arrangement a striking and welcoming display in any entrance hall, on a buffet table, or atop an occasional table. And the best part? With minimum care, occasional dusting and protection from direct sunlight, this display will accent your home with years of bright, beautiful, enduring color.

YOU WILL NEED

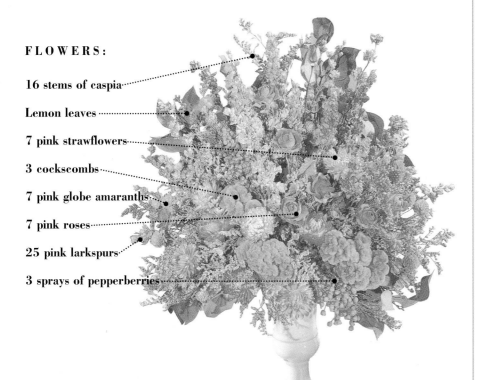

FLOWERS:

16 stems of caspia

Lemon leaves

7 pink strawflowers

3 cockscombs

7 pink globe amaranths

7 pink roses

25 pink larkspurs

3 sprays of pepperberries

MATERIALS: White urn • Floral foam for dried flowers • Kitchen knife
Sheet moss • Floral pins • Hot glue gun and glue sticks • 1 bunch of stub wire

1. Place floral foam into the urn and cover top with sheet moss. Establish the triangular outline of the arrangement with branches of lemon leaves. Add the largest flowers, the cockscomb blossoms.

2. Fill the side of the display with the taller stems of pink larkspur, loosely keeping to the triangular shape of the display. Add remaining shorter stems of larkspur to the front, spacing them evenly.

3. Arrange the strawflowers throughout the front and sides of display. Insert the globe amaranths in the same manner. Carefully insert the dried roses among the amaranths. You may want to wire rose heads for extra support.

4. If the sprays of pepperberries are very large, cut them into smaller clusters and attach a piece of stub wire to add length. Place clusters near the bottom of the display, around the rim of the container.

5. Accent the display with stems of caspia. Not only will they add to the fullness of the display, but they'll also provide a nice complement to all of the pink flowers. Fill any remaining holes in the display with caspia.

CLEVER IDEAS

Don't throw away petals that have come loose or flower heads that have broken off during arranging. Crinkle them into a pile of colorful potpourri and roll a small, glue-covered pitcher in the mixture. It will create a pretty adornment for any shelf or nightstand.

STUNNING TEXTURES

Accent a hallway with the sophisticated muted colors of dried flowers. Choose a classic-style urn and pack it tightly with large, dramatic dried flowers in rich mahogany hues. These stunning, shapely textures include:

- proteas
- mahogany-dyed eucalyptus
- hydrangeas
- strawflowers
- plumed celosia

PRIMARY COLORS

Extra-bright large blooms in primary colors look great all year-round. Bright yellow and red are the predominate colors in this sunny arrangement which is grounded by a complementary yellow vase. This arrangement of easy-to-grow, easy-to-dry flowers include:

- red zinnias
- yellow strawflowers
- daisies
- blue delphinium spikes
- lemon leaves

Victorian Table Accents

Flowers are a recurrent theme throughout the Victorian era and its ladies were known for their skillful tabletop floral displays. Now you can bring the elegance of that bygone era to your own table with these easy-to-make, yet impressive, floral accents that can be made in just a few minutes. Use them to adorn a water goblet, wine bottle, or a napkin. For a very special decorative touch, tie them to the back of your dining chairs.

YOU WILL NEED

FLOWERS:

4 pink miniature roses

2 sprigs sweet Melissa

MATERIALS: Wired ribbon • 1 pink napkin • 1 white napkin • 1 wine glass • Glue gun and glue sticks • Scissors • Floral tape

KEYS TO SUCCESS

● Lightly coat the ribbon you choose with spray starch to help it retain the shape that you desire.

● Add some fragrant dried herbs for added appeal. Try herbs such as purple and green oregano, sage, or even pretty lamb's ear.

● If you choose raffia or paper twists for the bow instead of ribbon, be careful not to spill food or drink, it will quickly stain the napkin.

TIPS & TECHNIQUES

● Iron your napkins flat before folding them to achieve a crisper look. Use a little spray starch for best results. If you're a little unsure about the folding technique, practice on paper napkins so that you don't crease the cloth ones.

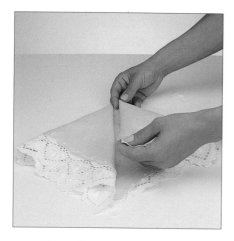

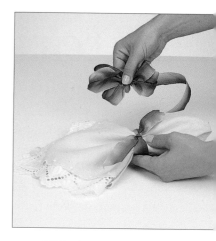

1. Place white napkin on top of pink one, overlapping by two inches. Fold napkins (as one) diagonally to make a triangle. With the fold at the bottom, bring both corners up to the top to make a square.

2. Flip napkin over so flaps are facing table. Cut about a foot of ribbon and tie around the bottom fourth of the napkins (not too tightly). The top part of the napkins should fan out a bit.

3. With about 2 feet of ribbon, make a simple two-loop bow. Tie bow onto napkin. So that your dinner guests can slide decoration off the napkin, don't knot ribbon or tie it too tightly.

CLEVER IDEAS

Plan the seating at your dinner party with lovely Victorian place cards. Start by folding a white card in half and piercing a small hole through the front of the card in the upper left-hand corner. Wire a flower to a small bow and slip the end of the wire through the card to secure it.

4. Using green floral tape, bind together a few of the miniature roses with the sweet Melissa. To hide the floral tape, you may want to glue another rose right on top of the tape.

5. Once the bunch of miniature roses and sweet Melissa have dried, gently glue them on the center of the bow on the napkin. (Be careful to glue the flowers onto the ribbon and not the napkin.)

VICTORIAN CHARM

Table accents in rich shades of orange and red will whet the appetite for an autumnal feast. Fold napkin in half and pinch in the center to form a bowtie shape and wrap ribbon around the middle. Use matching flowers such as:

- orangy-pink roses
- red rose
- purple heather

GOLDEN GLAMOUR

Start the New Year's off right with a bang and plan a holiday dinner party. Decorate your festive table with beautifully accented napkins. Creamy white flowers tied with a festive gold ribbon will set the mood for a snazzy black-tie celebration. In this design, we used:

- white rose
- statice
- heather

special techniques

DRYING FLOWERS WITH SILICA GEL

1. Select flowers to be dried just before they reach full bloom. Most flowers dried in full bloom tend to fall apart when dry. Use sharp scissors to cut the flower stems to within 1 inch of the flower heads.

2. Fill an airtight container halfway with silica gel crystals. Gently place flowers face up in the silica gel. With a spoon, gently sprinkle some of the gel around and between the flower petals.

3. Cover the flowers completely with some more crystals. Seal the container. Let the flowers dry for 2 to 7 days, checking daily to make sure the flowers do not over dry and turn brown.

4. When flowers have dried, remove flowers by tipping the container and pouring out some of the gel. When the flowers are visible, lift them out with a slotted spoon.

DRYING FLOWERS NATURALLY

1. Select the flowers to be dried just before they reach full bloom. Remove all of the lower leaves and trim off any damaged areas with scissors.

2. Loosely bundle a bunch of flowers together, about 9 to 10 stems at the most, staggering the flower heads so that air can evenly circulate around the flowers.

index